S0-BNY-978

BEYOND
the wire

POEMS
GARY GALSWORTH

Other titles

YES YES
A book of poems

BEYOND
the wire

POEMS
GARY GALSWORTH

CLOSED HAND PRESS
PORTLAND, OREGON

© 2016 Gary L. Galsworth
All rights reserved

Published by
Close Hand Press
607 NE 32nd Avenue
Portland, Oregon 97232
503-233-1784
ISBN
978-0-9798063-4-6

Book Design
Iwan Sujono
eOne Design eone.com.au
Editors
Aurelia Navarro and Janis Levine

Printed in the United States of America

Beyond the Wire

For the late Genro Seiun Osho with
gratitude for his friendship and his teachings
even at this moment.

—⁓—

Things are different since I watched the sun rise.
For instance
the day is beautiful today,
more beautiful than any other day
has ever been.
How is this so?
Things are different since I watched the sun rise.

Janis Levine

Acknowledgements

I'd like to recognize and express my gratitude to the following people for their critiques, suggestions, corrections, and especially their encouragement, loving support, and friendship:

Editors Aurelia Navarro and Janis Levine

*Trusted Reader*s Justin Millan, Peter Atkinson, Emily Turonis, Sydney Hoffman, Carol Millan, Hana Tierney, Olga Mederi, Eva Ninoska Camilo—and my exuberant cheerleader and sister ("all mouth and red hair"), Gwendolyn Galsworth.

Also, our book designer, from the land down under, Iwan Sujono.

And my Zen teacher, Soen Roshi, who said about life, "show up for *This,* as it is, no appointment necessary."

Thank You.

G.L.G.

Contents

Contents

TWO

many small stitches
bent against the rain

Contents

THREE

circles
things changed after that

Contents

Contents

ONE

the persistence
of hardwoods

...only knowing is left

Turning

It takes time takes a gap in sequencing
to let the light in
Don't hold your breath don't rush it
no
Turn it gently like the door knob to the attic

Once Inside

A couple of light taps and the door opened
looking inside I thought – mmmm
she motioned me in and asked me to sit
seated I asked to stay –
and I did
I do
we would

Longing
as in belonging
took shape in the room
a hand now familiar held
held tight
but not too tight

Inside the Walled City

In a room full of serious faces, I took my seat with a smile.
I believe it was the short walk in a sudden downpour that stirred it up.
And a recollection
of a walled city and a lover of mine... No, wait,
not the right words...we were lovers who possessed each other.
And at times,
there were times, when she would make small sounds,
like an infant. Coo sounds, goo sounds.
Joyful intense moments. The sounds one might make,
most intimately, in complete trust and dependency.
Yes, that would happen occasionally.

We lived in what seems now a walled city.
A solid block of medieval tenements, ours having
an elaborate entrance, from better days.
At the end of our block was a park, quite large and open, between
ancient plane trees.
A place by day where you could find a rundown bench, put down
some newspaper, sit and have your coffee and buttered roll.
The park was peopled by those who cared, and those who could
care less.
The "cared" would occupy and salvage a corner of the park,
to bring the kids to play in free of broken glass, and dog shit.
The "cared less" roamed, gathered, rested, got high, got excited, left
their trail of scraps and peelings.
At night, when the walled city had reabsorbed its people, the beings
of night evened it all out again.

Our three rooms were on the third floor. We lived in a naïve but serious
exploration of the day we had, and the day we wanted to make of it.
Our front room had a number of plants, thriving in the light and the
care my lover gave them.

In that care I did pretty well too, most of the time. Not having the receptivity, the willingness of the plants, I could also work doggedly at darkening a sunny day.

I see us kneeling at the back windowsill, close, snug, peering across the shaft and into the light of the kitchen a floor below.
The shaft echoed the metallic sounds of kitchens and the plain comfortable voices of women in familiar surroundings. And the cough of the sour old Ukrainian on the first floor, as he shuffled around his sparse, sad apartment, in his T-shirt and baggy pants.
Across the shaft and down one, in the bathtub, (the tubs were in the kitchen then) was a tall girl with long pale legs.
Blond hair, alabaster skin, the wife of our friend.
We were watching him wash her long legs, dutifully, affectionately.

Those two had been together since childhood, destined to
match and mate.
Later to have some boys.
But for now, under the yellowish light of the kitchen, he was washing and it seemed, thoughtfully yet tenderly caressing.
Not for the first time we watched and grinned and nodded
in complete agreement.

You walk on a path, late in May, and on the side of the path
you come upon a buttercup.
You stop; you have to, and drink it in. Lush, simple, perfect.
And you are in complete agreement.

Yes, there we were in the depths of this walled city, now dotted with lights and the sounds of its inner workings, enjoying each others nearness and the buttercups.

Before the Sun Rose

Before the sun rose I took my seat
after a while I got up
stretched
took a walk

The world had made such better use of the time
it had rained
and ahead a mushroom pushed up
through the leaves and shadows

Felt Before Heard

There is something felt through closed eyes
felt before heard
like the tentative sound of a chick still in its shell

The windows are touched
an inaudible presence enters the room
eyes open – to greet this day's falling snow

In Silence

This I saw, and it was seen in silence. The first it's ever been
spoken of is now.

Late in the night I opened my eyes and looked at the
woman. She was sleeping on the far side of our large bed.
She seemed such a long way off.
Though sound asleep her body was not relaxed, her face
set firm, too firm.
An effigy of some Anglo-Saxon woman.

Then I saw above and beyond where she lay a pale blue light.
Translucent, with reddish tints. I have seen similar color in precious
stones.
This light though had the substance of a veil and was a woman
floating weightlessly near the sleeper.
You might say, "Oh, he saw a ghost." But my mind was clear and
brimming with awareness. I never sensed ghost, but a visitor.
This visitor moved slowly without hesitation to the other and
lowered herself over and became part of her.
The woman, our love, did not stir as this veil-being encompassed her.
Like a butterfly alighting on a flower the visitor stayed only a moment,
then lifted away and at the edge of the bed vanished.

And in that moment I knew who and what had just happened.
Knew in that way where the "I" disappears and only knowing is left.
In this family, over a hundred years ago, an uncle had married an
Indian girl. Not so uncommon then. Her name was True Love.
An unhappiness had befallen her, and even after her passing
she had borne its burden.
She had come to this woman, her kin, who was good and trusting and
an embodiment of Love itself. Surely she could offer solace, refuge.

GARY GALSWORTH

Alighting, the butterfly understood. The flower was not ready, the nectar not pure enough, not potent enough, not yet, to carry them both to salvation.

The girl slept on, hardly moving, her breathing easier.
That she was chosen was a confirmation of everlasting longing and of the ripening.

Snowflakes Fall

Snowflakes fall
weightless numberless
upon the yielding pine

A Comeback

I think I'll make a comeback.
Looking up, after a long phone call with
an interested stranger,
I noticed this old cedar, crooked, shaggy,
and I became the interested stranger.

You Sit There

You sit there, like nothing much
is happening.
But I know, behind those dark eyes,
the honey runs.

The Moth

There's a moth in the shadow at the sidewalk's edge.
Like an old time biplane, a Fokker by its wing design,
it could take off, flying at treetop level and in no time,
land on that big stone downslope.
Be warm and toasty in the morning sun.

These stones have been here since the great volcanic blast
a million years ago.
And they have always been kind to moths. Offering a place to land
and rest.
Giving of themselves as, little by little, they are worn softly away
with each take off and landing.

A Monk

Between wisps of incense smoke
and that bright window
a monk tips and nods.

The afternoon moves west.

About a Mile

About a mile to get a coffee, cutting through the cemetery.
It's a Catholic cemetery.
The first stones are in Italian, from 1910 or so.
There were just farms here then and a few graves on the nicest
part of the hill.
Now the headstones stretch in all directions, almost to the main road.

On the walk back I cut through another cemetery, even older.
Early 1800s and Protestant. The first stones are just round-topped slate.
The etchings weathered to unreadable, or a faint *Emily... wife of...*
The newer ones will say *Beloved...*and *loving*. It's a comfort to see that.
Not much thought of death walking through here.
More, a putting of one's cares and worries quietly into perspective.
Ambition come to rest. Not a big deal in this waking of early spring.
Looking at the old church, all that's left of the village where once
Sam Holt devoted such energy to business, and family, in an America
just cleared of obstructions.
Or *Emily, beloved,* striving in the never ending labors of wife
and mother.

Up the road, and 100 years later, *Rosetta*, without a word other than
Italian, yet her hands, her whole body, expressing the heady dreams
of newcomers.
Entering the rutted track, I too bring my appetites.
After a few steps, on seeing *Father – John H / loving – Maryann,*
I am left feeling the bounty of *beloved*,
even etched in worn stone and long since reabsorbed.
How will I embody *Charles* and *Jacob, Anne* and *Julia?*
I read *born 1803* and feel the breeze moving across the grass and
stones, across the nicest part of the hill.
I read *died 1934* and hear the birdcalls.

The Open Porch

Through the blinds, not fully closed, a tree appears.
Substance and shadow, tossing
as it sleeps through another winter.
Its limbs are no longer capped in snow,
nor even the crisp leaves of a distant autumn.
All stripped away in this month of storms.

Seasons pass across the open porch.
Leaves collect in the corner by the rail,
snow drifts near the door,
wind and rain reach and soak and overflow the gutters.

Should I tweak the blinds another turn and give
the seasons back?

GARY GALSWORTH

Etruscan

Coming upon it in the tall grass, the Helm was like an old friend.
Cat's eyes cut out of heavy bronze, a broad nose guard, hinged plates,
the elegant sweep at the back of the neck.

Noisy panoramas rise up from a time before ignorance,
a time of perfect conviction.
A clash of spears and shields, the sun obscured in dust,
a place of desperate purpose.

In the midst of it again my heart beating against a mail shirt.
This place, past fear, beyond reflection. Unbroken contact.
This place of desperate purpose.

Lurid vistas flash past, stained, smashed frescoes.
Horses whinny, grunt, rear up. Great heat without sweat,
the fabled rush with no disorder. A clash of shield and spear,
and then

Long grass swaying in a slight breeze.
The Helm, suggested by a scrap of shell, remained,
speaking to a boy across two thousand years.

The Canyon Rim

A hawk soaring near the canyon rim
riding a far off breeze.
I can feel from here his unburdened heart.

for Sydney Hoffman

Parker's Woods

There was a sense of adventure, going down that road.
Especially after the pavement stopped, went to dirt,
and the woods thickened.
It was a long walk past Mr. Parker's farm,
past the fields he'd run us out of (small sweet watermelons).
A long thirsty walk, but once in the woods things
settled down. The tempo slowed, but the pulse quickened.
A sense of completeness and tranquility filled with quiet excitement.

I felt safe in the woods, strong in spite of the presence of the shadow
people, the running battles with them.
For I was also of the shadow people. Invisible, with that power
that comes from knowing. Looking into the trees, moving
through thickets, running down the narrow paths – knowing.

Once in Parker's Woods I came upon a full-grown woman,
sitting on a blanket, just off the sandy trail.
Sitting there in a white slip, leaning on one arm,
her head tilted and watching.

Dusk is deep green, turning to grey, rushing to blanketing black.
And all the sounds that black night is host to.
The world became small around the shelter of my old army
poncho and a candle.
A world of excitement went quiet, came close,
and just beyond that was everything.

The Woods Road

Walking the woods road
watching stands of fir and cedar
hold back the moon.

Escaping like silver fish
moonbeams flash past
winking their way to the deep and the dark

The Boy

I could hear his father crying, hear it across the stubbled fields
from back near the property line.
Bawling like a child.

And that was maybe twenty years ago. The boy was
ten years old, and the pain of his young life,
and his end of pain, were rising up even then.

Yesterday I called.
A caller, oh, another caller. His mother spoke to me
through clenched teeth. She recognized an old house guest.

A family crisis, a family crisis, she repeated. Even
through clenched teeth her words pleaded with the
listener, who was not me.

Perhaps a dark angel was being appealed to. Another mother,
another young one with a broken wing. These nestlings
with broken wings, plumage odd and in disarray.
They give you a shot at it. Take up an offer of help now and then,
before, shrouded in mystery, in opaque conflicts,
they take matters into their own precious hands.

Duality, duplicity, no road home are displaced by certainty,
unconditional acceptance, and love. All prevailing love.

Leaves

Leaves, each with its particular childlike curl,
lay everywhere. Crisp brown eddies that stir in the gusts.

Soon, a soft blanket will cover and quiet
each and every one.

Pebble

It's not that the pebble in my
sandal is not a friend
it's that starting with my toes
and now at the softest part
of my instep
it's been taking liberties

Behind the Plow

It's been 30 years now. Most of the crazies are gone, or in a few
cases, grown up.
Still, we'd be out of here in a minute, if we weren't so desperate to
get to the bottom of this.
The old man sits in his seat, delivering his message and instructions
on the mechanics.
Just the other day a few of us slept soundly through one of his talks.
I awoke occasionally to a chuckle coming from his direction.
Yes, we're still banging our poor unyielding minds against
his door, which he insists
is wide open, unlocked, or does not exist at all.

Determined we are, or we'd be gone. But then, where to?
Well in the best case: but there is no best case. Okay then,
in the worst case: but there is no worst case.
There is no case at all.
Only the old man's chuckle, tickling the hair in my ears, and I'm in
here sweatin' bullets.

for Shingen Jan Gaensslen

A History

There is a moment between breakers
as the waves seep into the sand,
where a curl of froth winds along the ocean's edge.
A marker, timeless and momentary.
The last remnant of a history
swallowed by the next reaching wave.
Beginning before dawn, outrunning the day,
breakers end their headlong rush
melting through this curl of froth.

Early Morning Tea

We gather around quietly for early morning tea
as small movements find their way into the dawn.
Movements that stir and spread,
as simple awareness seeps into every corner.
Purpose struggles with the willy-nilly
and we hold out for a second cup of tea.

The Bog

Seeds of anxiety sprout when I am made to be still.
And one wonders, worries.

That bog at the bottom of the hill, its watercourse finds a way
through the mud, the years layered in leaves.
Finds any way open to it.

Those fluids also course through the bogs and tendrils of my being.
Finding their way.
Whether I bow or rail, they go on in their honest work.

The Persistence of Hardwoods

Driving somewhere, it happened yesterday in fact,
and things will take on a familiarity.
Clues and cues suddenly adding up.
A line of hardwoods and firs, up on a ridge, roadside fields.
The way the forest floor is littered with tan and gold,
the way the trees tilt upslope.
Lines of stumpy hills, steep-sided, round-topped. Dark grey rock,
exposed and raw, cuts the highway builders made so long ago.
I feel like I'm there again, trying to make it be again.
The feeling of home, of having one.

TWO

many small
stitches

...bent against the rain

Many Small Stitches

Dressed in her light blue suit, presentable as always,
in the face of change.
Okay then, certainly beyond the possibility now
of cracking things open with an acid trip,
a "J" before meals, a love affair.

She told us once, "Really, it was like I was the oldest boy in the family.
The time we were crossing the Rocky Branch in dad's boat.
The river was up from the rains.
Jack fell in – dad didn't budge or say much.
Left me to fish him out and keep the other boys from falling in too.
I doubt I ever got over that one."

In the slide show, there she was, even as a child,
always a toothy smile and her arms around a couple of scruffy brothers.
Looking right at you, like you were what?
One more thing to do?

We had a comfortable, if brief, friendship.
I felt she let me cross the moat,
opened the gate and welcomed me onto the threshold.
We shared that space and in that small space
breathed easily.

In the chapel, looking at what they had done,
which is after all what they do, I thought, "Naked.
Just lay me out naked, imperfect teeth and all.
Or wrap me up in one of your quilts."
That's the way, but it wouldn't fly would it.
Like this, do I know you?

We wanted her story. The details. Her window into that experience
when everything was done the old way.
Plowing a hill so steep only a mule could manage it.
Five kids atop that same mule, snuggled close
for a Brownie Hawkeye pic.

Wouldn't tell it though. Something she could not prepare
for, put in an appointment book, got her along the way.
One of those ogres in childhood that comes off the page, out of the
woodwork when we are most defenseless. Devours and digests
a part of our history.

The unscathed, the fresh, keep asking. Find it interesting,
irresistible.
The also-scarred leave us be.

Last night her sister and I slept under one of her quilts.
Deep blue and light blue flowers, flecked with red and white buds.
Ebbing and flowing across powder blue fields.
In the evening, in the soft light, we slept under fields of stars,
as powder blue turned to clouds of nebulae.

I would love to have laid that quilt on our apartment floor.
Sat there, invited her to share the magic carpet.
And now she can, can't she?

1/1/09

Squinting through the blinds
the porch thermometer reads 19 degrees.
Last night's biting wind is gone,
carrying with it many foolish thoughts
from the old year.

I'm sure they'll be back soon enough,
tapping and rattling my windows.
For now, a cold clear night
grips everything outside.

In here a candle flickers.
The arm on the wall clock clicks
with each small movement.
And an occasional breath of mine rises up.
All partners to nothing in particular.

Hurricane

The thing about a hurricane, about a flood, the thing about the filth,
the mountains of sodden possessions growing on sidewalks, in the
streets –and it's still raining! – is it tells us, dragging another heavy
bag or end table from homes now more hovels – to let it go.

Don't look back for a third bitter time. Don't look too far ahead, and
don't look back, not right now. You don't have to.
My boots are half-filled with water. I'm too busy to pull them off and
empty them. What for? Wet is wet, they'll just fill up again.
It's greenish, this water, from the ocean and the river, from the street
and below the street, from drowned cars and oil tanks. From all of us.

If there is a lesson, it's in the socks. Mine are a terrible bother,
clammy wet, slippery and falling down around submerged ankles.
In all this, right now, I could do without those cold clammy rags
embracing my feet.
Reaching for a box which disintegrates at the touch – all funky – and
in the wetness, a picture, so tiny by comparison, of our child or of us
as a child.
Damaged, smeared, but you know, peeling it away, it might dry out.

One of These Days (I)

Rummaging through a box of odds and ends,
cleaning the apartment for a second time.
The first was just after he passed.
That large bottle of aspirin, I remember putting it in here.
Now it sits beside the coffee can of Bosco's ashes, bottles of
vitamin C, assorted pens, eyeglasses, an old magnifying glass.
Our family dog, in the end his dog, relegated to a box of odds and
ends in the basement.
A box of leftovers from his master's life.
Should I throw out all those pens, and the vitamins are not that old.
I remember him using the magnifying glass reading his mail.

Mr. Gorman lies in another can, across town, in the storeroom of the
funeral home.
They've been good enough to keep him till the family gathers.
We've talked about it twice, briefly.

It comes to mind, would it be okay, do you think, to one day take
a pinch of Bosco's ashes and a bit of Gorman's ashes and sprinkle
them on Ma's place in the cemetery?

In our old rooming house, Mr. Gorman had kitchen privileges.
Ma made sure he had his own refrigerator, pots and dishes.
On occasion he made a meal for us. His specialty was corned beef
and cabbage or a roast with mashed and peas.
He'd serve the meal with a grumpy pride but never would
sit down and join us.
We'd ask, insist, but no, he wouldn't give in.
The informality would have changed it for him.
Ma made sure he had his privacy, almost a separate home within the
house, though they all shared Ma's last years.

Bosco always near at hand quietly stealing all the attention he could. She'd say, "He's not a dog. When he looks at you, he talks."

That big kitchen.
My mother would wash the floor, then spread newspapers over it.
It made no sense to me. Newspapers all over the place, getting under foot, shredding in the traffic. Protecting the clean floor.
I actually used to ask myself, and others, what's the idea, this room, ankle deep…?
Some old Jewish custom from Flatbush or Bensonhurst?

We've been talking about a memorial service for Gorman. About planting a Japanese maple.
We've agreed that everyone loves a Japanese maple.

Soup Bones

Sitting in a diner, and there's a group of teenagers, laughing,
chatting it up, bouncing off each other's energy.
Someone should tell them, give 'em a hint, don't you think?

Making the rounds, sorting out the day, all was more or less okay,
till the doctor threw an x-ray up on the screen.
"What's that!?" I cried.
Coral? All porous and underwater.
An ol' soup bone, tossed to the dog ages ago, turned up by
the lawn mower?

His suggestion, same for his assistant, is that that is me.
Impossible!
A lie.
As likely the tree trunk dissecting the window be me as this object,
worn, vulnerable, evolving and eroding, without my awareness,
without my consent.

At the front desk, I wrote out a check and left.
For all appearances acquiescing, agreeable.
But I'm not done yet.
I'll think of something.

And I Love a Story

I could tell you about people, someone hammering on the other
side of the property.
Can't see him, except a mental picture I have, a man bent in the work
with tan overalls, a cap pushed back with a curved bill.
Then there are the girls in the kitchen. I can hear them too, laughing
and talking to each other.
People are interesting, their variety, their meeting of interests.
But with them come tears.
Smiles as well, yes, but it comes around to tears.
The pain of change, the pain of things staying the same. The stories,
some grab you in the stomach.

I'd rather tell you about plants, grasses, insects buzzing through
weeds and flowers.
I'd rather talk about the shrubs and bushes, full of summer, dappled
under green and yellow saplings.
Watch how a breeze moves through them.
There is no heartbreak in an afternoon breeze pressing warmly
leaf-to-leaf.

Picking Me

A field near the side of the road
filled with flowers
I'm not much for knowing them
but it was a rich picture
a tapestry of violet and purple
with a number of yellow daisies

Stepping across a ditch
then through the weeds
I found myself amongst them
and it was a daisy I noticed
as if we had been looking for each other

Without planning to without meaning to
I bent and chose this flower
tucked it in the band of my hat
and headed back down the road
In a short while
a whisper said
thank you for picking me
I was sure of it

Then I took the flower from my hat and
placed it carefully in my shirt pocket
where it stuck out like a friendly greeting
more than one passerby said "nice flower"
a lady remarked "I love your daisy"

How did it come to this – crossing a roadside ditch
to stand amongst them – walking home

wearing a flower
Crossing the porch I looked down and saw
the flower was losing its brightness

Finding a glass in the kitchen I filled it with water
and put the flower in the glass
it helped
what more could be done
Ahh – a bit of sugar in the water and
it helped
The daisy came back and on the windowsill
brought a radiance to that corner of the room

By evening this day's gentle acquaintance
was leaving
I won't describe the changes – which came as
a surprise – or how for a while I was lost in them
As this shared day ended we looked again at each other
and the breeze whispered
thank you for picking me

Wet

Caught in a downpour,
feeling sorry for myself
bent against the rain.

The streaming pavement passing underfoot.
And a yellow jacket is walking across it, soaked like me,
heading for the nearby bushes.
He's so dignified, businesslike, in his efforts

I straighten my shoulders and
find a little joy in the warm driving rain,
even some comfort in tugging down the wet brim
of my wet hat.

Stone Still

And you, because of my love for you,
I sit stone still.
The snow wraps its white coat around me
and streaks my face with sweet water tears.

The Two-Day Blow

A fast moving river of wind rushing beyond its banks.
Rushing and drowning all other sounds.
An invisible river, pushing and bending great trees,
giant ponderosas.
High up, branches bent round, whipping, streaming,
like the hair of wild-eyed mermaids riding out a gale.

Branches that never straighten, curved for life,
not unlike the sharp-turned mountain roads below.
One formed by knuckles of grey rock,
one by a hundred years of impassioned caresses.

The grounds, the paths, raked clean just yesterday,
are covered with pine boughs and brushwood
from the torrent's passage.

Gone now.
So quiet you can hear the twigs and bark crunching underfoot.
A spectacular parade swept through, took up the whole high valley,
like a boulevard in some great city.

Now, to the quiet relief of cleaning the litter
and walking upright.

In Amber

She was sitting on the stairs, and she was worried.
Below in the kitchen, three adults,
none of them her mother or father, but two aunts and an uncle
were arguing over who should take her for the next few weeks.

Small, quiet, sitting above the living room,
hoping they would not notice. Hoping to be invisible.
Quite possibly they would not have cared if they had noticed.

She didn't like staying with any of them, was uncomfortable,
anxious.
Why did this have to happen, why did she have to go...
And a bigger question. *What if none of them would take her?*

That was the first she remembered of a course of events
that had started long before.
But this one memory had crystallized:
softly lit stairs, the living room below,
bright light coming through a kitchen door,
edgy voices from the people inside.
Now all held like a dragonfly in amber.

Good Night

I said good night but didn't mean it.
I meant good, the night.
I meant come over here,
on to my arm,
and into the light that slips through the blinds
so I can, and you can too.
Fair and bright, babies all grown up,
so you can be one now,
in this good night.

for Carol

Running

The sound of running feet, driven by what urgency,
called by what hunger?
I, sitting over here, the stars in their silent multitudes over there,
the runners pass between us.
Till their sound, biting into the path, slipping on
loose stones, fades and gives way to a shifting electric hum.
The dialogues of the insects of night.

Rock Amongst the Rocks – A Ballad

You never gave the ring back and never said a word.
A mystery.
My niece put it in a nice way–your reasoning–and I left it at that.
It was better.
I'd have just taken the ring down to the Rocky Branch and thrown
it in.
Over by where that walking bridge used to be, long ago.
Better.

Word would have gotten out about how this fellow was upset
and threw a 7,000-dollar diamond ring into the middle of the creek.
Kids would be wading in the shallows, with sticks and rakes,
looking for treasure.
Before long there'd be serious adolescent expeditions in
waders and rowboats.
Searching and yelling over to each other, what they're gonna do with
the money, from that crazy Yankee's 17,000-dollar ring.
Then their big brothers, fathers, and sisters would join in. Just the
thing on a nice Sunday afternoon. "Let's take the boat and go find
that rock in the middle of the Rocky Branch."
"It's said some rich New York Jew fell for one of our girls.
She was a real one.
He courted her and got serious.
She got restless, uneasy.
When she gave him back the ring, he drove all the way down here
and tossed it, all 28,000 dollars' worth, into the Branch.
It's said to be not far from the knoll where her daddy and
her kin are buried.
Then he turned around and drove his long way home.
I've heard, after that, he never was quite right."

You never gave the ring back and never said a word.
It was better.

True Love

I saw you the other day,
and you looked right through me
no recognition.
Just what I have hoped for
looking at me, you see no one.

With a Child's Hunger

Stroking her hair, thin, silken, kept so clean here.
Does she know my name? She used to say it often.
Often, just for the pleasure of it, it seemed.
Now, no name is on the tip of her tongue.

Brushing the hair from her eyes so I can look into them.
Let mother see me look at her.
Tilting forward, our foreheads touch. A familiar nuzzle.

I'd love to see a smile, but she may have forgotten about smiles
for now.
There is a murmur though, full of inflection and trust.
A part of me understands perfectly.

As always, our meeting is brief, for she has things to do.
As a child I'd tug on her dress. She'd look down, speak to me,
a few words. Caring, gentle.

I craved more words, a tide's worth, a heavy snowfall on the
meadow's worth.
Tugging on her dress. But our meetings were brief in that big
kitchen where I'd be on the edge of so many important things.

Now amid so many reclining souls, little islands of passivity, inert
and quiet, she's off.
Dragging her locked wheelchair, gripping the floor with curled toes.
Down the corridor. Things to do.

A child's hunger for more, more time and more words,
is still in me.

I feel the pull as she moves away and hear again the murmur
we shared.
Somewhere in that murmur, that language all her own,
she knows my name.

for Opal

Halos

Watching snow fall through halos of street lights
it's been snowing since early
seems for years
used to be things that moved me
got to tell her – wait 'til she hears
now she doesn't care to listen
let the snow fall
onto my hat my face my shoulders
let it pile up
to melt – when the time comes

Heedless

A friend of a dear friend
was killed last night
in the wreck of his 18-wheeler

I keep thinking of him
at the bottom of that ravine
as I try not to step on the ants
rushing heedless under my sandals

After

After the hurricane, scattered tree limbs
and a wreckage of boat hulls litter the tidal marshes.
Acres of reeds, their furry tufts still intact,
bend and sway in a steady breeze.
On the radio a piano playing background
runs through riff after riff.
And people on the east side of the city gather in an
anxious, sorry crowd,
for handouts of food and water.

Pleasant Dreams

Ribbons and small dolls fill an old basket.
She says, "I just want to show them to Mom."

A tan woman, crinkly from age and the sun,
her hands the hands of a gardener.
A big garden, stretching into the meadow behind the house.
Now all blanked over with tall grass and dried stalks.

A mind gone elsewhere carries tokens of interest,
pliant textures, soft pastel scraps, her brown basket.
Clues and cues from unquenchable childhood.

"Mom, where's mom?"

Overgrown

Looking for a place to sit or set a notebook on. Not easy to find.
This house, overgrown with boxes yet to be sorted,
bright ideas crowded out by brighter ones.
An apple here, almost ready, a book there, almost read.
Papers atop piles of papers, full of promise,
too interesting to throw away.
The yard with grass too high and weeds higher. Trees not trimmed,
stretching to catch the sun.
A face overgrown with stubble, hair down to my collar.
Baggy pants sagging, the mirror nagging, I seldom look.
My mind overgrown in chains of thought, filled with the ambitions,
the appetites of a nesting bird.
A life overgrown with history, reflections of me and needs to be.
All set aside by these eyes of interest.

Streets

Streets with their comings and goings.
But where is a sign of her passage?
Will she spend the rest of her journey beyond contact,
beyond recognition of our time in this thin place,
this world of life?
The one, the other, living it out without words.
Out of hearing, out of listening. How can that be?
Not even the smallest remnant of you and me.

I walk down the street, she's not on it.
It goes up the hill to a grassy lot, small houses,
children in a driveway.
Empty.

Rain's coming, feels like rain, any minute now.
We'd have talked about that, looked into it.
Are we to miss this opportunity of the coming rain?

And of her hair, so much, in shades of red and brown.
I cannot find even a single hair of hers on a sofa,
a pillow,
in these many rooms.

I know this is all true, because in my dreams
walking up the hill past small houses,
I can no longer find the right place.

These streets with their comings and goings.
Rain dripping off porch roofs,
flower beds soaked in it.

The true thing is, I thought it was her absence,
it is her presence,
at the end of every thought, in everything I see,
that finest trace is you.

Dog-Eared

Can one's life get dog-eared?
Perhaps it's time to water
the hanging plants
and go to work
on that old maple stump.

Florida

After Pop died Mom would visit him in the cemetery.
Sometimes I'd take her and leave her alone sitting on the grass,
talking to him.
Mom wouldn't say "cemetery" – one of her foibles – she'd say, "I'm
going to Florida." or, "I'm going to visit Dan in Florida."

She called him Popsi-Doodle when we were little children and on
the morning he died.

Love, plans for the better – salvation even – and family, in a war zone.
Well, all gone now.
And so the other day I went to Florida.
Brought flowers from the yard, roses, dandelions, lilacs, for Ma
and Pop, and a few for Mimi.
And also for Mimi, the usual, a cup of Duncan Donuts coffee, and
a French cruller. Except they were out of French crullers, so at our
daughter's suggestion, a Boston Crème.
Walking along the winding paths, a friendly landscape, could be on
a calendar.
Reading the headstones, the little sayings and comments, and what
was big for the person passed. For the men, a lot of info on Army
service, WWII, Korea, the Fire Department.
And about kids, love, heavenly hosts for the women.
Finally, sitting on the slope next to Mimi, this time I took the time
to figure out what side of her simple headstone she was on.
I had it backwards for a while.
Talking to Mimi, giving her updates, remembering more clearly
than ever what a decent little being she was.
Talking about our child, now with her own life and family, its pain,
dreams, struggles, between sips of coffee, bites of donut, ruminations.
I finished my share, laid the rest down for her.
Not far off a man was also visiting a loved one. He was standing on

one side of the plot, then shifting to the other side, holding a prayer
book, or some small volume, and praying or chanting.
Christian, Hebrew, I couldn't tell.
It got me to looking around at the vases of plastic flowers, made so
perfectly nowadays, and the tall glass jars with a candle burning inside.
And here and there, miniature landscaped perfections around
a headstone.
Finishing the last of our coffee, I saw how we all find a way to pray
and touch something in this place.

"You are my sunshine. My only sunshine…"

Memories, sweet, bitter, are absorbed in that first taste of Boston
Crème, or finding one's place again in Kaddish.
A place beyond tears and sorrow. Tears or joy enter in "carry out" only.

Sitting on the grass, playing all the parts, putting life back into them.
And many of us that can smile, do.

Seeking Nothing

Every day sitting quietly – seeking nothing
yet seeking rises up
I can't help feeding it – but I feed it less

THREE

circles

...things changed after that

Beyond the Wire

I consider my father a hero, shit that he was
in many ways.
What he did, what he didn't do,
left, came back, ran out, but came back.
Looking out, beyond the wire, it'd scare the crap out of
anyone.
But he kept the secrets he was sworn to keep. Kept those,
the big ones, the ones you could beat someone to death with.
And he told us his stories and answered our questions, which
we asked again and again, in our delight with how he answered
them.

An inspection by professionals may have found him wanting.
A bit of an imposter, a house with only three sides and holes in the roof.
The rest a fill of plastic and tarpaulins.
But even incomplete, a bulwark.
The gaps filled with expectations, memories, lies.
That bulwark behind which children feel safe from miscellaneous
predators, roving bands of Huns, the loud, the hungry.

Halloween-like, ancient history has been seeping up out of
the damp ground.
A streaming of phantoms, pointing and gesturing.
I feel obliged to answer for him.
Heroes don't leave their posts.
Pop did.
But he came back, picked up rifle and bayonet (a child's rubber bat
would have served) and proceeded into no man's land.

Possibilities

You are right in what you say
you are precisely – well –
generally right in what you say
shouldn't we try anyway
meet where we can
and help each other leave the rest alone

There are possibilities here
for genuine affection
and serenity
lively interchange and –
affection
if only we don't get too alarmed

White Truck

A long time ago we had horses.
Frosty, a cute little s.o.b. of a pony. I got him for my daughter.
He was fine to look at but, as is often the case with ponies,
nasty to live with.
He never threw her, though he tried. He threw me regularly.
And Indian, a tall old white horse. The kids loved to bend down and
walk right under him.
He didn't bat an eye or lift a leg.
One day Frosty charged a stone fence, the kid holding on like a rodeo
rider. She didn't know the danger.
S.o.b. Frosty went back (for far less than I paid) to penal servitude
and plain hay, no grain and molasses at the local riding stable.

Time came to leave our little farm, return to Queens.
We tried to sell Indian. He had a lung condition, he wheezed.
No buyers.
A great disposition but an embarrassment for the kid who loved him.
Youngsters love their horses, it's a fact, but she rode with girls who
had "good horses."
They would be out on the roads and trails, her horse would start
wheezing till it went over to the sound of impending heart failure.
She'd have to pull up and rest him.

One day a tall slightly stooped old man and his wife came by.
Said he'd take the horse.
He was in retirement, wanted to plow some land behind the house,
till it, the way he used to as a boy.

His wife, though not enthusiastic, was agreeable.
I told him about the "condition," the wheezing.
Not a problem, we won't run him, and – oh, you are
worried. No don't you worry, I can't work that hard on
my end of the plow. We'll be okay.

GARY GALSWORTH

Recently, driving to the post office, on the side of the road,
a white truck for sale. One just like I used to work out of.
Had it set up just about right, a great truck it was for those years.
I'm not working like that now. Couldn't sell it, paid to have it towed
and donated not long ago.
Today I stopped by and walked around that little "for sale" van.
Thought about how I could set it up, about how I still get a call,
now and then.
Might feel good to have it sitting alongside the house, ready to go.

Only a Dollhouse

Inside there's a dollhouse.
And inside the dollhouse,
I'm bouncing off the walls.
On the brink of losing it.
On the brink of torching it.
Might do myself in,
in the smoke, the flames.

It's only a dollhouse.
Exists only
in these ruminations.
Can't I open the windows,
crack the door,
let the dog out?

One Day

One day they'll come for him and haul what's left away.
Then someone else will come and nose through stuff.
Read a page, take in a letter, remark on a picture, a lamp, or,
"This guy sure had a lot to say. An opinion on everything."
Is this an antique? Worth what?
And that old shopping bag of drawings…
Lord, this can of loose change is heavy.
And who'd have guessed he had so many pairs of shoes.

Then there is the rest –
Him sitting quietly in the front room, drinking bergamot tea out of
a glass jar.
One of a set of mason jars his son had sent after he explained,
complained, how that morning his jar had cracked pouring hot
water into it.
Sitting, sipping, listening to the sounds outside.
Morning birds, the wind, morning people closing car doors, driving off.

Listening to small sounds inside, house sounds as it heated and cooled,
lifted and settled. As it minutely expanded and contracted.
Sitting quietly, listening to the sounds of his own inner works. Webs
of thought, colorful meandering sequences, passing breath and those
many moist processes within, as they minutely expanded and
contracted.

Listening to, sensing, the flowing clouds of matter that life had clothed
him in.

Airborne

Megs, 6, and I, old, out on the porch watching the comings and goings in the street.
Her hand in mine, we decided to wait for you out front.
Cosmetics, composure, an outstanding entrance. No end to details.
Watching you around the house, more naked than not most of the time, was a treat.
Dessert between meals, in a messy kitchen, a disheveled bedroom with too much furniture.
Skinny, pale, a hungry waif, in North Jersey's version of "God's Little Acre."

But my patience was leaking away on your getting ready.
In this case, going to your sister's wedding, where, with screams and howls, a brawl with the groom's friends awaited your besotted brothers.

You called, I came inside, looked up.
At the top of the long stairs, dolled up in a light blue dress.
It went with your eyes and hair.
Bare shoulders. Lots of dress and heels.
Yes – looks great.
Easy now, we'll get there on time.

About halfway down, your heel snagged.
Or your hem. Or our wacky life caught up with us…
You tripped – and sailed into the air like a circus performer.
A natural, face forward, dress and legs stretched out behind you.
Airborne.

Our accelerated life, perennially on fast forward, slowed way down
And you sailed the last eight feet or so, without haste.
A look of complete surprise, but not fear, spread across your pale pink face.

I raised my arms, caught a fluffy bundle, and gently set you down.

Megs had a question or two on what had just happened, and why? Answering her with a hug, I realized, that in spite of our apparent disarray, the slightly sordid, lightly soiled complexion of our lives, we were cared for.

after Frank O'Hara

Epic Morning

That summer my summer job was in one of the big resort hotels.
I stood in front of a deep sink with a large drainboard on either side,
in an out-of-the-way corner of a busy kitchen.
Waitresses would bring in trays of dirty glasses, set them on the
right-hand wing,
and the glasses would move through the glass washing process and
wind up on towels, upside down, on the left wing.

My job, a glass washer in a resort hotel on the shore.
The operation outsized me, was out of scale for a 13-year-old boy,
but the job got done.

After a while I got more comfortable, more at ease, and started
keeping an empty gallon jug under the right side of the sink.
When a glass came in and the drink was unfinished and not messed up
with lemon seeds, cigarette ashes or cream, I would pour it into the jug.
There was your grenadine and vodka, brilliant red. Your bright lime
and yellow mint juleps, your tan Long Island iced teas. All went in.
Also leftover whiskey sours, martinis, gin and tonics. Secret fun it was,
and by the end of the evening almost a half-gallon of honey-colored,
alcohol-laden fluid got collected.
I'd carry it home balanced on the crossbar of my bike. Give it to my
friend, the old guy in the second floor rear of my parents' rooming house.
He was grateful for my remembering him. He'd pour himself half
a glass of the concoction, and down it went.

No pause or thought on his part about germs or like that. So I didn't
worry either. Not that I had any interest in taking even a small sip.
The complexion of the fluid would change each evening, depending
on what drink was most popular that day.

The most interesting and nicest thing about that job was the kindness
and care shown me by the waitresses, many of whom had growing
kids of their own.

And, that in my corner of the big kitchen, I was out of the mainstream. The rush and pressure swirled and eddied around me, but I was safely off to the side.

One day at the start of breakfast, the head waitress came into the kitchen in a real sweat. The cook was drunk and couldn't cook. His assistant hadn't turned up at all.
The hotel guests, who were being seated, were beginning to order. Oh my! "Can anyone cook breakfast?" she asked.
Everything stopped. I remember it like a kids' game where at a certain word you have to freeze wherever you are, even in mid-step, arms held out for balance.
The waitresses, the busboy, the dishwashers, salad boy, the manager looked at each other, from one face to the next. Like in slow motion, shaking their heads; no, no, not me.
"My god, breakfast is now being served, but there's no one to cook it."

When my sister Gwen and I were about seven or eight years old, my father gave us the job of cooking supper. One week each, on a rotation. And he also taught us to make eggs and pancakes for breakfast on the weekends.

I could even flip over-easy eggs. You know, flick the pan, the eggs go up into the air and over, and if things go well, if you just do it and don't think about it, they land softly and safely back in the pan. Omelets, I had learned that too. Folding them over, folding cheese into them.

Oddly, I could not get the hang of scrambled eggs. They stuck to the pan and were a mess.

In the roar of the silence of the hotel kitchen I spoke up, "I can cook eggs, I do it at home."
Heads turned, looked at me in astonishment, in relief. (and: *you got to be kidding*)
The head waitress came over and leaned very close in a motherly way and asked was this really true, did I think…?

I said, "Sure, I do it at home."

There was a pause, then a moment of universal agreement, and the kitchen sprang into action.

I was practically hand carried to the big black and stainless steel ranges and grill. A couple of people became support-the-cook assistants.

And so it came to pass that that breakfast in that New Jersey shore resort hotel was cooked by the glass washer, who cooked the eggs and pancakes to order. The toast and garnish, the fruit cups and all the niceties were handled by the rest of the staff.

Everyone was very patient and supportive as I worked my way through the orders. You could order whatever you liked from the menu, and you got either sunny side up, over-easy, or an omelet. No scrambled. Sorry, no home fries, no Eggs Benedict.

Depending on what the order looked like in the cook's head is what you received. So Eggs Benedict became an American cheese omelet, as did scrambled eggs soft.

Over-easy was easy. I missed only once, and they wouldn't let me clean it up, but said, *it's okay, okay, don't worry*. Handed me another skillet and turned me gently back to the stove.

We got through breakfast. The guests, many of whom got wind of the special situation in the kitchen, were pleased in their own way. The waitresses whispered encouragement and smiled. And I stayed busy. Whatever was ordered, you got what was closest to "the picture," and pancakes. Sorry, no french toast. At home french toast was considered fancy food, and we never made it.

Later, and for the rest of the season, I was okay, contented to stand at the big sink, washing dirty glasses, keeping an eye out for reusable unfinished mint juleps, and whiskey sours, letting the busy business of the kitchen swirl around me.

I also enjoyed the knowing smiles, in passing, that occasionally came my way.

Days Go By

Days go by, talking to no one,
and the conversation never stops.
What's more interesting than that?
Even the cheap seats are sold out.

Inconclusive

Pop used to dig holes in the backyard. Big ones.
Ma would say, *"He's in the yard digging.*
He's going to dig all the way to China one of these days."

A picture would form in my mind, among the mind clouds it would
shape itself:

> A hole through the Earth a bit bigger than a man.
> Brown dirt sides, not rough, not smooth.
> It went directly through the Earth.
> Pop digging away, until suddenly,
> there would be light breaking in on the far end.
> China.

So I'd put my school stuff away in my room, if I had my own room
at the time, and head out back to see.
There he'd be in that big hole. Easy to understand Mom's concern.

"Pop, what's this one for?"

And he'd explain about drainage and breaking up the clay barrier.
He'd eventually fill the holes with old bed frames and bed springs,
and pipes and junk. Then shovel in dirt and plant a couple of
fruit trees.

We had a big backyard with clusters of fruit trees here and there.
The trees seemed to do well if they survived all the surface commotion.
But there always seemed to be more to the story.

Sometimes I'd look at Pop and see him with a mustache,
and he'd look like Hitler. Was he?
They said Hitler was still alive and out here somewhere.

A picture would form – among the mind clouds –
I'd start looking for Nazi-in-hiding behavior.

It was inconclusive.
I never asked. Never pressed for more info.

Did lots of work around the house: my chores,
but was never told to help dig the holes Pop dug.

Another reason to suspect there was more to the story.

The Old Black Chevy

Pop was a bit hard on me, so I'd run away.
My sister Gwen would meet me secretly at the side of the house,
with some bread and a can of tuna.
Then off I'd go.
Usually after a day or so Pop would come looking.
If I was in Parker's Woods, forget it, he couldn't find me.
In the old abandoned golf course, even with all its brambles and
hideaways, it was easier.
One day, having evaded pursuit, I was shuffling along, muddy and
at loose ends, when I saw Pop's old Chevy on the dirt road.
It was one of those prewar sedans, very black and square.
And I remember, it didn't have a tin roof like other cars, but the
center of the roof was made of tar and some sort of canvas and wood.
I used to think, wouldn't it have been easier to just make the whole
roof of tin?
You couldn't climb around on a canvas and wood roof.
Anyway, I see him and start running like the dickens. I can still feel
muddy cuffs hitting my racing ankles.
But I couldn't outrun the old jalopy, and soon Pop drives up along
side and says through the open window, *"Where you going son?"*

The Sheik of Arabie

My father was a chef
Liar!
My grandfather was a tailor
Double Liar!
My mother was, was…
Wuz not!
When I grow up, I'm gonna be
Yeah, Right!

gonna be…

Circles

Things changed after that,
I started noticing first buds, the sweep of branches,
a spring breeze.
Even how cars lined up at the curb, one after the other.
Started noticing, taking note, slept on it so to speak.
Got the picture without looking for anything in particular.

Pulling my hat against the gusts, I see how grungy the lining is.
If I wash it, I can't wear it till it dries.
Would anyone notice an old guy wearing a wet hat? Rivulets running
down his temples.
Probably not. If they noticed they wouldn't care.
Relax, people don't give a shit on the trivialities.
You worry about such trash. They got other things going on in
their heads.
It's a hurricane in there.

Things changed, changed up, but I couldn't say how they were before.

Tea and two slices, Orwell used to say. *Tea and two slices.*
Don't fret, it's all not much more than a frown darting across the
moment, like a small quick bird.

I understand, we all want our song to be sung, want someone to
notice before the tears dry completely.
Frankly though, not one bud will be altered, not one cloud will
devolve differently.

But that's not the point either is it?

The Lizard and I

Meeting on the path the lizard and I
jockey and shuffle
until – with a flick of sand – he breaks for the sunlight
at the edge of my shadow

Brooklyn

Born in Brooklyn. That's what I tell people.
I'm not sure. Seems unlikely, but I'm not looking any closer.
My mom's family had a rooming house in Bensonhurst,
her dad is said to have frequented the burlesque.
Her mom, a heavy-set woman, is said to have disapproved.
Ma and her twin, both perfect for their day,
had dreams of becoming dancers on the stage.
Vaudeville.
Not allowed of course.
I tell folks we came from Williamsburg.
Now full of artists and professionals, then full of poor Jewish families,
who for the most part did not know they were that poor.
The kids found out later.
Let's face it, later we found out a whole lot.
Juicy info up the wazoo – later.
We found out way too much and were probably at our best
thinking a big round orange all for ourselves was the real deal.
The rest of the story is how I spent the rest of my life trying to get laid,
trying to work out the crick in my neck (left side) and figuring how to
play it, read it, think it through, so the people I wanted to, usually the
same ones as in item one, would recognize my realm for what it was
and always would be: the center of everything that mattered.
A hard sell.
Frustrations, storms here and there, some big ones when you
need 'em least.
To date they've been weathered, and I've stayed interested.
As interested as a kid bent over his radio, listening to the game
in Brooklyn.

The News

...and I had secret hopes she'd call

The news of your marriage snapped open that album of pictures I'd
finally put almost out of reach.
The winds, balmy and stormy, of our time together turn page after
colorful page, and with each picture a tableau arises – atmospheric.
I don't try to stop them, but sit and watch; outwardly
quiet, inwardly not so quiet.
The news is a blessing though. That improbable phone call will now
never come.
And when this dies down to a breeze, the album will be moved
to the back of the shelf again.
Maybe a little higher up, maybe a little farther back. Maybe.

Mom Takes a Swing

Shorter than I even then, she beat on my arm with the side of her fist.
Determination, and a familiar frustration showed on her face as she said,
"You will listen to your mother, do you hear?! I won't tell you again."
Which she had been telling me again for some time now.
I was about 13 then.

As a child I was unable to resist cutting across a lawn, balancing on
a wall, jumping on a bug, which would set mom to stamping her feet
and yelling (actually, since we were in public, hissing energetically)
for me to get back over there and walk next to her.
My sister, round, red-cheeked, did not have the same need for
independent forays, but walked along side her mother, comfortable
and compliant.

At 13, beating on my arm did not bring the desired result, so mom
hurried away with short serious steps and came back with a broom.
And proceeded, with her face scrunched up, to bang on my arm and
shoulder with the broom.

It didn't really hurt, and I couldn't quite figure what her plan was.
I was half dodging the blows and peering down at her with an odd
look when she caught my eye, and we both started laughing.

Teakettle

The teakettle has started whistling,
and it's getting louder, more strident.
Making the bed, I plop onto it.
Sink into the thick cover, absorbing the sound,
with a certain peace of mind.

The teakettle insists.

To get up, something will have to start moving.
Legs, torso, my arms.
A body, half buried in warm sand,
being called... starting with what part?
The feeling is sort of wooden.

Ignored, a wailing sets in and sets my heart thumping.
The rest of me is relaxed. And tired.
Sleep is elusive these days.
It used to embrace me and I it
for prolonged periods, content, submerged.

Serenity is starting to fracture
in the face of the teakettle's relentless call.
But a struggle will gain little traction here.

My favorite bedtime story flashes past.
You are holding me, your arms around my chest,
your breasts pressing against my back.
Even the teakettle's wail softens
in the recollection of your arms and breasts.
A niche, settled into night after night,
as a cathedral of closeness and sleep arose around us.
Existence, at the farthest end of the universe
from this insistent alarm.

Get up, get up, move; if only for sweet tea and milk.
Living steam wears on wooden limbs.
Like the faithful dog in stories, it wants only my response.

FOUR

technicolor

... a fragile barbarity

A Short Leash

sniff and root
having it my way

there's that dog in me
have to keep him on a short leash

I don't ask you to look me in the eye
if you'd rather not

nor ask you to stand up naked
on the far side of our room

on a short leash
the dog waits

The Glint and Cast

Out of the dark, darker than pitch,
the glint and cast of intelligent eyes.
Watching.
Watching the wheels of thought and premonition
roll into pictographs, psychodramas.

Who knows, something may turn up out there yet.
Likely as not, sweaty cul-de-sacs, low budget reruns.
Don't we owe it to ourselves to wait and see?

Our shot at knowing that last handful of aborigines.
Warriors, maidens, timeless grandfathers with bones through
their noses.
A fragile barbarity, living it out, on the far side of the regions.

Intelligent eyes looking out of opaque worlds.
Black irises in creamy pools.
Ageless connections.

Our shot at seeing things askew.

The Day I Got Stabbed

It was like in the old movies: the scruffy kid looks up, stops in his
tracks, his jaw drops, his eyes get big as saucers at the sudden
appearance of a ghost or something spooky. Then he spins around
and runs like the dickens!

I'm 73 now but can see clearly the train tracks, the gravel bed
speeding under me as I ran looking for something to defend myself
with. And also beat the crap out of the little black kid and his skinny
pal who were chasing me.

They had been picking on Marshal Prairie, the sole employee of the
"Ice Cold Soda" business my sister and I had. Run from a homemade
stand outside the racetrack parking lot. We actually sold a lot of soda.
Sis screaming like someone possessed, *Get Your Ice Cold Soda Here! –
Get Your Ice Cold Soda Here!* All mouth and red hair.
On hot days we sold a lot of soda.

Marshal and I were also friends. He was a well brought up, quiet but
eager kid whose parents moved a lot, 'cause his father was in the Army.
I was the protector in our friendship, being a little bigger, but mainly
because I was always willing to fight.
When he told me about getting pushed around, I went in search
of our enemies.
I found them, two black kids from downtown.

We had words and went to look for a good place to fight it out.
The railroad track, seldom used, that ran past the Race Track seemed
good enough.
Pretty isolated.
So me and the smaller kid, about my size, but the more aggressive of
the two, started to fight.
I hit him a couple of times, 'cause I was into boxing, when he called
to his buddy, who threw him a knife. A switchblade, with a narrow
pointy tip.

And he holds it up, says something "big shot" threatening, and stands there waving it from side to side.

I said to myself, OK, can't fight a knife, don't know the tricks, so I gotta run and find something to pick up. A piece of wood, a beer bottle, a good sized stone, something! I turned around and started running, searching as I ran. But I was sore about running away.

In my code you don't run (except from my father). In our neighborhood gang, led by Earl Bennet, who could climb any tree and fight anyone and win, you didn't run. I can still see stuff along the tracks as I urgently looked for something usable. The other kid not far behind me, calling me chicken, a yellow belly, and like that. There were railroad ties strewn here and there, bags of solidified cement, big branches, beer cans, newspapers.

But not one useful thing.

OK, you can't keep running, forget it. There is nothing. Can't lift a railroad tie or a bag of hardened cement; and this kid thinks I'm running away from him.

Time to stop and fight it out.

So I did. I stopped and started to turn, and the kid ran into me!Bam! He jumped back, knife in hand, and I got ready. My mind was open for any number of possibilities.

Then I noticed the "scruffy kid from the movies" routine. Especially, "eyes got big as saucers," and the kid and his buddy started running away from me at full speed, yelling to each other, pointing back my way. I couldn't make sense of it.

I just happened to look down after a few moments and there, my left arm was covered in red. Like I had a red sleeve down to my hand. Odd? Eventually I understood it was blood, and wet, and my blood. There was a warmth to it.

The kid had sunk his knife into my arm when we collided.

I walked back along the tracks till I came to a gate that led into the racetrack parking lot.

There was a guard in a shed. He came over.
I said something about something, and he opened the gate and took
me to the first aid station in the racetrack.

After some initial commotion they calmly cleaned me up and bandaged
my arm, asked how I felt. The hole was deep, but not wide. The medic
said it was good to bleed with wounds like that, for cleaning, but not
too much.
Then the police arrived.
I must have looked pissed, betrayed, because the medic told me he
was sorry, but, with incidents like this, they had to call the cops.
A detective sat down with me and asked me for details.
I told him I was sorry but couldn't rat anyone out. After which we
had a long, intense conversation in private.

Eventually they let me leave. I walked across the big parking lot,
down the tracks, to home.
Pop was sitting in the kitchen. I could see him through the window
holding his newspaper.
He listened to my story, felt the arm, the bandages, and asked if
I was OK.
Then he suggested I do not tell Mom I got into a fight on the railroad
tracks and got stabbed.
I see so much of this clearly, especially the flight along the tracks, the
railroad ties strewn at angles off the grade.
But I can't remember what sorry story I told my mother.
She wouldn't touch the bandages but held that hand, toying with my
fingers as I stood there lying to her.
And she brushed my cowlick off my forehead, but it fell right
back again.

It Did Rain

Like the desert wants rain, thirsty for it,
that's how I want you.
It did rain. The pure joy of it.
Rain sound on the roof, cool drops on my face,
the scent of grass as it freshens.
That's how I want you.

As you walk past, a hidden smile between us.
Is there a promise of rain in that smile?

Paired

A quiet rush wept out in a moment or two
for who – with sadness still – not quite
more like the geese I believe it's them – that mate for life
whose mate has fallen from the sky

only an instant ago beside him
laboring on their joined journey
taken for granted two in one
two into one complete ever changing always complete

fallen away – to where
when
he can not begin to ask
now embodies both yet she is missing
feelings come unbeckoned

as he flies on – part of that great 'V' we find so charming picturesque
a hint of the faraway come near
of course the ranks close up
an aerodynamic necessity known to them
the same way paired is known the flock complete but not

the gap
a missing beat of wings a missing voice as sweet as dawn
from that high place
and through this gap fall tears
longing
finds us as we look at familiar places – our favorite things
then all becomes insensible
discovering oneself without the means to comprehend

GARY GALSWORTH

to then move on
and find a place in the order of things

without exception dawn appears
a new entourage each morning
day brightens takes us by surprise
the absence of our own reflection

surroundings blur – horizons vanish
take care that no one sees
their concern and all
how can they know I am not alone

then to smile and find a place again
in the order of things

That Moment

Don't you feel like we could eat each other up?
Eat you and all the space around you.
How long would that last, not long I'm sure.
Maybe a bit more than a moment.
But in that moment, the living in breath and out breath of you,
the humidity, the clear eye of you would be the bounty in my chest.
Finding expression and life in my fingertips, on my lips.
Yet I would be rootless, without a source,
my existence swallowed whole by you.

Don't you feel that and know for sure, if we looked into
each other's eyes and our eyes said yes,
we could eat each other up?

Technicolor

The top of my heart broke off
the bottom of my heart broke open
and all the jelly beans spilled out

177 Morris

It went down in front of our old rooming house on Morris Avenue.
They stood toe-to-toe, eyes dilated, nostrils flared, raging and
indignant.
Ugly words, spittle flying back and forth.
The tax inspector was much younger and about a head taller than
the old man.
And the inspector was at his wits end, almost out of control,
and was saying,
"Listen, if you weren't so old and bent, I'd knock you on your ass
with one shot!"
The old man, his face scrunched up, his eyes piercing, pointed
a finger into the inspector's face.
"Old ! Old you say! You know what I'm gonna do?" he said.
"You know what I'm gonna do? I'm gonna shit on your grave!"

"Can you imagine!" my mother said, "Of all people for your father
to get in a fight with. And to say that to the tax inspector."
"I tried to stop him. Get them apart," she said, "Hopeless. And the
awful language!"

I thought, not for the first time: where does he get this stuff?
Maybe from being European? *I'm gonna shit on your grave.*
It's good.

A Wren with a Crumb

Itch itch
Fingers reach to intercede
finding one's nose with a certain
parental concern

Then the itch flies away
like a wren with a crumb
intent on mischief elsewhere

Prince and Wooster

The dial above the elevator doors moves slowly from floor to floor.
It stops, and the racket opening the inner gate reaches me through
the glass of the entrance.
The elevator doors slide back and out steps my escort.
He sees me peering into the lobby and smiling his usual whole-face,
whole-hair smile reaches up and lets me in.
When a visitor shows up, Little's family job is to run the elevator
down to the lobby and then escort the guests up to the family loft.
If they are new guys (the family has lots of visitors) someone will
inevitably say, *Wow, you run this old contraption all by yourself?*
Little's answer is always about the same.
Sure
If his sister, a bit older, gets off the lift, you know right away that
Little is out, sick in bed, or grounded.
Hey, hi, I say, *good to see you*
I don't say, *You sure have grown since...*

Little is his nickname, though not because he's little. He's average or
maybe a bit taller than average. It's because of his father, whose
nickname is Big.
And he is. Tall and fit, a large presence, a big brain and sculpted
red beard.
All quite heroic, which I believe Big is somewhat convinced of himself.
A self-absorbed fellow, wrapped pretty tight, not the stuff of heroes.
(Whatever that might be.) I believe he means well.
Does one have a choice in being "wrapped pretty tight"?
I love his wife and their two children, so have tried to bond with him.
Took it as a challenge over a scotch or a joint.
After a time, gave it up.

Little and I are comfortable; some small talk. *How did Cornell's show
turn out?* (Lives on the third floor.)

Mom says he sold a few paintings, and he's very pleased.
Mmm, pleased, I say.
And is little Ed (truly little) still trying to get a date with the new girl in the back loft?
Wow, Little says, *Mom asked me the same question yesterday.*

He doesn't have a prayer.
Spoken with the finality of an insider.
Really, I say, *How come?*
I'll tell you, but you and Mom can't tell anyone.
No problem, we know when to keep a tight lip.
His teeth are too yellow, and she's pretty. So, no way.
The verdict; and it can't be appealed.

Caught up, I shut up and enjoy Little's expert handling of the levers and gates that let this old crate go up and down.

The Apology

Our fathers were both Swiss, unlikely as that was.
Drawing a bead on a fat robin with my old Daisy pump action.
His father Germanic, from Zurich, mine French, from Geneva.
It was a pleasure, a wonder to hear my father speak French. Effortless,
and the speakers understood each other, completely.
Pow! The robin dropped right off her branch. Delighted and aghast
simultaneously. In my excitement I'd shot her outside the kitchen
window, the window still closed.
My father always beat me in English.
And so Danny Tanner and I had another resident for our animal
cemetery.
Dan lucked out, his turn to be the preacher.

An apology to Mrs. Robin, I say that sincerely.

As a dive-bomber pilot I was determined and relentless and could
carry the war to the Japs, right through lunch.
They'd find me out front, on the sidewalk with a golf ball, bombing
red ants, large red ants, into specks. Reddish irregular specks,
sprouting antennae and wirey legs, against the rough grey of our
concrete battlefield.
Dozens of direct hits; immersed in dive after exhilarating dive, but
the Japs kept coming...

An apology to those innumerable fallen.

The youngest kids in the caddy yard, usually also the smallest, were
the last to be picked by the caddy-master. So we passed our afternoons
at the edge of the stream searching for turtles and frogs and other
living things to kill in unspeakable ways.

Demons of the underworld, as you drag me off, deservedly no doubt,
let me look back and shout, "I am sorry," for what and how we did
– to those poor innocents.
Sorry!
What little monsters, psychopaths without remorse. In fact, what
joy in the hunt, the relentless search, the appetite for unblinking
destruction of life and limb. A tribe of baboons, hyenas, predators
that favored Clark bars and baloney sandwiches.

In the hottest, dampest part of a humid afternoon, I brushed away
rivulets of sweat, and aimed the 50 cal. at three old women, crouching
as they crossed a hillside field between the paddies.
How close could I come?
Two fell to their hands and knees, as the monster bullets sprayed dirt
and brush over them.
The third stood and looked toward me, far up on the opposite hill.
A look, a stance of no nonsense, of lost patience,
of "Son, think seriously about growing up."

Just Being There

I can't figure it, don't know where to begin.
Don't even want to know.
The girl, some neurotic shit to work out (if she wants).
It's one of those times where you just got to leave it be.
Let it recede, get worn down, like glass in the sea.
Right now, the edges are too sharp.

There were butterflies though;
butterflies when I'd see her.
Big ones, bright, and little ones in pastel shades,
fluttering inside me.
Miniature hang gliders, ecstatic in just being up there.
Without thinking much about it, there still are.

Via Caravaggio

An antidote to retreat via hidden streets
between walls via secret stairways –
to an attic
raw and leaking November winds

There is a chance – the voice of children
heard in some predawn corner of my brain
heard still – not coming through the window
not rising off the porch

The voice of children – no matter
may draw me out into daylight again
Ponderous body now at rest
cares come all undone

Obituary: Love Prevailed

He held her pinned beneath a three-legged stool, like a serpent.
But she was no serpent, just a slim muscular girl,
writhing and twisting, reaching up with sinewy arms,
to grab, to claw.
Her teeth were bared under curled lips,
and she screamed at him.
He muttered and grunted his reply.
Her brown red-rimmed eyes were filled with rage
and joy.

Death Is the Beginning

The *inji* scolded, "You are getting thinner and thinner,
shrinking away like the oldest of grandfathers."
He may have raised an eyebrow. Doubtful he acknowledged her
more than that.
" If you die soon, you will leave many of us adrift.
How fair is that to those who have been with you all this time?"
She spoke in Japanese, so the content of the words had more flavor
and portent than I can render in English.
It was ok, she had always been adrift in his realm, in the sea
of his cosmos.
He sipped a thin soup, ate half a chunk of soft chicken and asked
for tea.

These followers had been instrumental in keeping him alive and
viable.
Until recently, he had been grateful for their commitment, their love,
their various ambitions. Now sitting propped up in a chair like an
infant, swaddled in layer upon layer of white robe and under-robe,
all of which hung large on his wilting frame – now staying viable was
a toss-up.
Thin, thinning man ate his thin soup because it hardly mattered,
and because he still loved his work.

Just recently, on meeting, he pulled me to him, I figured for a kiss,
or a carnal gesture.
Instead he stuck his finger in my ear and whispered,
"No, only receive."

Bowing to leave, I tugged on his big toe, clad in a soft white sock,
a bit more gently than usual, and backed out.
Glancing up, I saw him looking at the cottonwoods in the yard,
with the freshness of a child just out of doors.

Not Saying a Word

Great things looming
But they'll have to keep
I'd rather sit on the floor
My back against our bed
And watch you slip on your socks
Your hands smoothing the tops
Against pale ankles

Fired up – lots of things in the works
And you know what – help yourself
I'd rather sit on the carpet
Leaning on one arm
Watching long nimble fingers
Adjust and tidy important matters
Under your dark skirt

Great things looming
The world outside calls me
To bang my chest against it
And get the business done
Not saying a word
I'd rather watch the belt at your waist
Study how it captures
And holds your blouse
As you move across the room

Silent both of us as if I weren't here
Was absent and you alone were preparing
To enter the cold morning
Breezing past our window
A crinkle in the corner of your mouth
A crinkle in the corner of your eye
Says directly to that place of appetite
Of yearning
You – You – who are not here

I Wish

I wish I could place my hand against her face
and tell her how much I love her

It's not so easy
and sometimes that makes me mean

Iwo

I sat staring absently at the screen door that opened out from the
pantry to the yard.
A cross brace intersected the door's frame and held a fascination.
My attention though was mostly on the voices coming from the
kitchen.
Listening to the four men seated around the table, smoking.
Each with a small plain glass of red wine in front of him.
They were talking about the war.

We were all still inhaling and exhaling the war.
The landscape of our minds and awareness continually reinventing it.
Turning and probing the details, the experience.
I was little, seven or eight, and of course loved everything about that
all-consuming adventure where we went in as and wound up being
the indisputable Heroes.
Certainly in our own eyes.
And I was, without a doubt, one of the Heroes as well.
In fact, even then, I couldn't wait to grow up and join the Marines.
Needless to say, on my Iwo Jima there were no young Marine's
entrails being ground into the ash and sand.

My father sat among the men over by the window.
As the conversation intensified, gained in somber but colorful energy,
I realized there was information I could contribute.
My father had grown up in Switzerland and northern Italy during
the First Great War.
He and his friends played on one of the innumerable battlefields in
the mountains of northern Italy.
During one of their escapades, Pop picked up an explosive, probably
a small detonator, that blew up in his hand. It made a mess of it.
As Aunt Marie said, "I can still remember Donato's beautiful hands,
and then that explosion."

He had a normal thumb and forefinger and most of his middle finger. His pinky was all gone and about two-thirds of the next finger. And there were scars.

In our family little was said about it, but it wasn't hidden either. Pop had one hand with parts missing because of the First World War. That's what I told my friends, who would notice and later ask.

I stood up from the little table in the pantry, the one where Sis and I ate, and carried my bright idea into the assembly.

My heart was full, my back straight; here was something significant to report.

My father could measure up with the best of them.

Warm in that knowledge, standing next to Pop I reached over and lifted his hand, saying clearly, "My father was wounded too."

That moment detonated into another explosion, and I found myself tumbling and reeling back into the pantry. Somehow finding a stunned seat at our little table again.

I hadn't figured on Pop reacting that way. Violent disapproval hadn't even occurred to me.

The picture had been a nobler one.

This quest for a part in the war, for recognition, backfired and got me knocked for a loop.

Dazed, staring at the screen door again, its cross brace and turnbuckle holding a fascination still, even through the blur and bewilderment.

I was not crushed, not like that poor Marine on Iwo, but it felt bad.

A big reversal.

Something good was supposed to come, something grand.

The opposite had happened.

Earthquake like. How does it go? A 6.5 is many times, not one time, greater and worse than a 5.5.

Something like that.

Nevertheless, inside I knew my father had been wounded in the war.

Vespers

Bare feet press the wooden floor
We meet as friends.

Outside frost descends, black night and bright stars
look down with crisp familiarity.

From deep within eternal warmth rises
and coats the galaxy in dew.

Fingers flex to reach and touch.
A toddler moves from uncle to cousin,
from treasure to treasure.

November's Forest

Trees spike the air
like hair in heavy metal
but quietly

Slopes curve away
rising brown and wheat
absorbing the colors of dusk

Stiffness tension drain from my hands and shoulders
late autumn smoothes the furrows in my face
and I am handsome once more

One of These Days (II)

Hosing down the porch
washing off the last bits of leaves dirt dog hair
remnants
Flushing them into the yard with blasts
of cold water
It's been weeks of steady effort to clean and scrape
bleach and paint away
the imprint of Mr. Gorman and
Bosco's last years in their apartment
Washing away these last bits and pieces
last odors and markings
It comes with a certain sad relief
like looking back over the stern of a ship
long ago
my home receding over the horizon
I was not unhappy to leave yet felt the
loss in the center of my stomach
Today these mixed feelings are overtaken
by a presence that still pervades the house the porch
the yard
an agreeable presence that turned a cranky old
misanthrope into an accessible laughing person
Bosco – limping around up and down the porch steps
nosing in and out of this room and that
with a shambling enthusiasm till the end

It's true – dog piss saturated the carpets

the floor tiles
ate into the wood flooring

The apartment almost uninhabitable
I thought I'd have to tear the house down at one
point
It's true Gorman cried an awful lot after the
dog died
Died a bit later perhaps than was best for all involved
After that I'd come over clean the house some
throw out the overdue garbage wash the overdue
dishes
mutter and grumble to myself then go shopping for
this broken-hearted old man
His shopping list used to be pretty fair
always about $50.
Without the dog just a couple of things
He wasn't interested
And it's true he collapsed onto his funky sagging bed
his heart stopped at an inconvenient time
Out of town they handed me a phone message
and I remembered giving him a kiss on a whiskery
cheek just a couple days earlier
Remembered the tickle and itch of whiskers
the softness underneath
What a pain in the neck
well not a pain really just painful decisions
on the next step the what the how

Of course it all unfolded and wrapped itself up
as these things do

including someone taking the $700 wad
out of his dead man's corduroys
An impulse to get very pissed
but then just let it go
I want to tell you it was all okay
It was without a doubt just about right
And so thanks to all involved
even through the last of the last act
No curtain to draw or take down
just go shut the hose and change my shoes
they're wet
Of course – of course there are no ghosts
of that twosome that passed through time
in this old kitchen
but there is something

Honey Tea

Reaching for the glass
of tea and honey
expecting one last swallow
but the glass was almost dry
barely a trickle
and that was better than ever

Perfect

Glad to have worn a scarf and the heavier jacket.
I'm in front of the stationery store where we agreed to meet.
Opening doors for someone carrying a large folding table.
Visiting a city that is no longer my city.
And that's okay.
It's getting colder as the afternoon wanes.
Without burdening this with too much thought,
seems she decided not to wait.
Okay too.
Our fourth meeting, but my heart isn't into it.
Was reading Faulkner on the train. He set the mood.
A twilight place, in place and time.
Across the street, across the broad lanes of Sixth Avenue,
it's bright and full of contrast from the sun.
This side is in afternoon shadow.
Details tied together by the twilight.
My heart's not into it, but if she came around the corner,
there'd be a happy gripping of arms and hands,
lively affectionate hellos, faces peering into faces.

What the hey. My depth gauge is obviously broken.
When it was working I wound up heading for the rocks
just the same.

Not now, but once, there was Elsbeth.
A young girl who'd visit me every week or so.
Breaking out of a marriage that had gotten drab.
Whose more colorful fantasies, anticipations, had been just
out of reach.
With me she grabbed them.

Would show up with long auburn hair, loose down her back,
and in short leather skirts.
Our weekly music lesson. Turning my little spot on the heroin-funky
Lower East Side to someplace in Paris or Trieste perhaps.
A risky serenity embraced us.

One day she said it had saved her marriage: uptown somewhere.
Another day, a year or so on, I walked her to within a block of
the subway.
We turned to each other and, after a gentle affectionate kiss,
said so long.
No words, no debris, hardly an echo.
A warm day on a street corner. The music lessons were done.
Perfect.
Today the chill is working its way through my boots and jacket.
Perfect.

A Matter of Fact

I must have been 13. Sitting with my father, listening to his take
on things.
You know I hardly sat with my father.
It was more a being in his presence.
When we looked at TV, a couple times a week on special days,
I would sit with him.
Watching "Victory at Sea," sitting side by side, was like that.
On this day I was listening to his comments on assorted subjects.
When he wasn't raging, being a psychopath, he was about the most
interesting person in my life.
He punctuated a point saying, "Now remember these things. I won't
be here forever. One of these days I'm going to kick the bucket."
When he said that, so matter of fact, everything stopped. Time,
movement, froze.
It had never occurred to me that he could die, that he would die.
Even then it felt a surreal prospect.
He must have seen my look 'cause he added, "Really."

Eventually he was, as he so often was, right.

Beyond Is...

From a small niche illumination shines
its message
belief in something akin to stubbornness
akin to hope
a Dairy Queen swirl of it

Those days seemed long and many
he played hunted frogs and snakes
made new friends
teased or annoyed the girls
and waited
knew what he knew

Sitting quietly hands clasping one another
a playful feel in the face of life's procession of losses
waiting
a character flaw he probably always had
it does not look at odds count probabilities

Outwardly mute accompanied by a lively inner
knowing
evening breezes picking up cooling
flagging his shirt sleeve – that too
its fabric blended low-keyed

A sense that if one can be still
quiet and willing in ways that are
beyond patient
then of course she will come back reappear
find him

She must mustn't she it's obvious
one need only look out from that tiny
illuminated niche
she's walking down a long driveway
turning every few steps
so they can wave to each other – till she is gone

Those days seemed many
he played hunted
made new friends
waited
knew what he knew

enormously pleased when she came back
enormously pleased to be together again

You ask *what if?* and that's a good question
though birthed in a different realm
so you may find this confusing
and that too makes sense

I am also bewildered an avalanche out of nowhere
of opacity perplexity a thug
yet this knowing – waiting – lives in prehistory
in places before bewilderment
so the question never comes up

No Place No Space

There's no room for you and yours
no room for me and mine
There is room for breezes to whisper
for branches to bud and brighten with leaves
Room for a carpet of blossoms
deep blue and pale green
to push up through the earth
still chilled from the night
No room for you
and no room for me
Room for patterned yellow flowers
that cover the quilt
our warmth trapped beneath it
Room in the darkness
for blind feet to meet the boards
and find their way
Room for early light to cast up the hill
raising the trees on its crest
to their starkest and tallest
for song at the edge of the wood
where grouse and turkey
are making their rounds
Room 'neath the plum tree 'round yesterday's
porridge
for cardinals and sparrows
the squirrels that chase them away
Room for the clothesline stretched over tall grass
on down to the brook that runs past the barn
Room for a picture of us in our heyday
Afternoon smiles the meadow behind us
Room for a whisper or silence
The breeze on the hillside
and into the treetops
no place no space
no you no me

It Plays Out

Danny Whitley walked arm in arm with a friend,
gave those closest reassurances, a thin smile, and went his way.
He used to play the piano for us, his special thing, when we were
little men.

Mom waited, seemingly asleep, to feel her children near.

Mimi needed to scold me one more time and exchange kisses
with her child.

It plays out,
and the pieces change alignment.

FIVE

new music

...a simple rightness

How Things Fit

Have you noticed how things fit
a band of sunlight on a wooden floor
leafy shadows from the cottonwood outside
flickering over it

Just clearing the highest bluff
the sun is far too strong to look at
but can be seen in all its brilliance
in the roses by the railing

for Mik Hoffman

On This Familiar Path

On this familiar path
how many stones have
felt the weight of footfalls
how many footfalls the weight
of time

Dust and the sounds of passing
mix and are set free
to rise and settle again

My ears are becoming deaf
to it

In the Distance

Walk down off the knoll along the rocky trail,
then across a footbridge and on to the boundary line.
Stand amongst the boulders and undergrowth, not to hide
but to blend,
and some days, in the distance, you'll see a woman, maybe two,
threading their way through the trees.
Mythical creatures, just out of reach.

An Old Cabin

Atop the hill sits an old cabin. A small one. It might sleep three in
a tight fit.
Hand-hewn sides, boarded-up windows and doors.
Except for one small window.
Peeking through it, into the gloom, you can see a couple of sleeping
platforms and a high shelf along the wall. There ought to be some
canned goods stacked there. Cans of hash and stew and string beans.
In the back, the dark shape of a wood stove. Its decaying chimney
poking up through the rear wall, reaching above the roof at a tired
angle, rusting in the drizzle.
I'm relieved to see the roof is still intact, keeping the cabin's interior
out of most of the weather.
Along the roof's northern edge layers of moss cling and thrive.
The cabin's front porch is caved in. No longer able to carry the
weight of the curious.
Let's try that door. Is it locked?
A path carries me around the cabin. Past the cordwood rack with
a few pieces of wormy wood still stacked.
And on the window ledge, old soda bottles, heavy, embossed, right
out of childhood.

What more could one ask?

One to the Other

Geese fly by. A quick pull and they glide out of sight.
I can still hear them calling.
My own wings are sore, especially the left knee, but both
are showing wear.
Things gets pushed and pushed a little harder.
Nearby, in the fork of a sugar maple, a squirrel, soft in its winter coat,
goes through small moves.
Nibbling, scratching, and altogether on the other end of the elegance
of geese in flight.
Except its lush tail, trembling with each movement.
As lovely as a fine muff held lightly and warmly in St Petersburg.

My step sets a grey pebble tumbling toward the edge of the road.
Then there is water over stones, sounds like glasses being touched.
And bark laying around in strips and little heaps where it has
sloughed off a fallen tree.

Good Thing

The heart of an artist is a soft heart. Whatever the exterior,
and I've known some hard cases, real pricks; it can't be otherwise.
Like the heart of George, my original father,
a soft heart in spite of the hard exterior of his life.
Unyielding– not so much him – his journey.
His heart stayed soft, supple, willing.
See, he had been taught to make bread by his mother.
As if she knew.
Good thing.

for George Weigle

Once Upon a Sunny Day

Standing in the middle of the world. The middle, it seemed,
of all things.
A dime held tightly deep in the pocket of her dress.
Looking down she saw her shoes had gotten dirty from the walk.
Holding her father's hand, she had tried being careful of the muddy
spots in the road.

Licorice, two in fact, she decided, seeing it blossom out of a glass jar.
A licorice flower.
All around her, great, slow moving figures. Overalls, work boots,
cigarettes.
A friendly gathering, her father easy among them.
In that crowd of boots, shifting, stepping on a smoke, tapping to a
conversation, she could always find him.

Quiet joy, an eager face, licorice and the corner rack of magazines.
Passing the men, who bowed her way, smiled, and asked in a word
or two about familiar things.
She could not answer, did not quite speak their language this morning,
but smiled upward.

Then, eyes to the plank floor, she moved along.
Her Mom would not have let her look so closely at the magazines.
Look through that window to a distant, an exquisite world beyond
these trees, these mountains, and these big men. *In boots they
haven't kept clean.*

On the center page, the blue ocean, waves, a wide wide beach.
All sounds become the ocean's sound, she kneeling in the sand,
in the bright sun, eyes round and clear with discovery.
Soothing, the voice of her father coming across the waves,
Watch love, don't hold the page too tight and mar it.

A soda pop. That leaves two cents to bring to Mom.
Pennies for our penny jar.

Fingers nestled in that safest of all places, that hand like soft leather,
her bag of licorice held tight, they walk along the roadside.
Turning her head towards the store, its red sign calling for another
walk and a soda pop on sunny day with her Pa.

The Pacer

Some forms of violence come easy,
but instead of coming out swinging,
I paced the room and bit my lip.

Some schemes for retribution come easy,
no problem. So justifiable.
But instead of finding the means, the cudgel,
I sat on the edge of the bed,
clasping and unclasping my hands.

Time was when hurtfulness, proactive and prolific,
was natural. Digging holes in the back of our yard
now seems the obvious thing to do.

Surrounded by lies, errors, and miscalculation;
safety and relief seemed only my due.
Taking a lesson from the heroes and mythical icons,
I planted three emerald evergreens,
and waved at our grumpy neighbor.

I Suppose

I suppose
for dreams we could bank on
for time we considered our own
for the life we knew belonged to us
what it would look like
taste like feel like
I suppose that's the origin of chants and requiems
clearly thought-out articles of faith
denied
I suppose the *New Yorker*
the *Economist*
why not the old *Village Voice*
will comment on conditions
as they were supposed to be

An Easy Breeze

Wind bells chime
new shoots bend
in an easy breeze
and taking the stone steps
my knee says
slow-ly

Imperfect

I.

It's an imperfect world, though some people
have very good parts; *you have a perfect nose,*
like that.
I had nice hands. People would say, *Oh, you have nice hands,*
long fingers, you'll be a pianist.
Actually I was a boxer early on. Fairly good at it,
but my hands were small and kind of delicate,
for punching the shit out of someone.

II.

Seeing my shadow against the wall,
I hadn't realized my head was that small, my neck that long.
Square shouldered, but had I gained, getting thick around the middle?
Just when you thought...
I took a deep breath and moved on.
My shadow stayed put.

The Lost

The sky darkens holding a promise of rain.
Can't you catch the scent?

An umbrella, faded but still colorful,
dangles from its owner's hand.

The wind is shifting, no longer from the east.
With it dark clouds lighten and move out to sea.

Intermezzo North Jersey
(waiting to get you)

Leaning against the car, an eye on the door your class lets out of.
People watching, thinking of you inside brushing your hair,
collecting your stuff.
A joy in it, a simplicity.

The door swings out, and there you are, just after the first.
Arms full, handbag, yoga mat, another bigger, brighter bag.
We'd joke on the volume of indispensables a woman needs
to leave the house.
Chatting with another girl, both your energies up, a pleasure to watch.

Looking up you see me and smile, big smile, meeting and holding
my own.
And with a little jump, you lift your hand and say, "There's my man."
A joy in it.
Moving across that space toward each other, a simple rightness held us,
an obvious truth.

Your man no longer. What seemed clear became clouded, oblique.

On occasion I sit back and let that afternoon come over me again.
Let a smile wrinkle across my face, across closed eyes.
And I still believe in the truth, the freshness of that day.
That afternoon, waiting to get you.

for Mary Allen G – Mara

Musing

The chipmunks took a liking to me today. They kept showing up
here and there.
I was leaning on the bridge rail over the bog, musing – you know
and from under, on a bridge beam, came one.
I looked down at him, he looked up at me.

Nearby, a maple sapling is growing out of the bank.
Its leaves are broad and a deep autumn yellow.
One leaf detaches itself with a delicate finality,
like one's very last heartbeat, and flutters to the ground.
When it touches, it makes a soft sound.
A falling leaf landing amongst the other leaves does that small thing
so well.

And with the sound my companion blinked, and I blinked back.

Thinking of Soen

"We really should keep on with the poems,"
I said to a thick root, stepping over it.

The root agreed, its gnarled fingers having supported
men and weather for countless seasons.

An authority like that, my spirits lifted,
and I looked for a place to sit down.

Confessional

In a confessional just below his navel, he stood
naked, hairy, round-shouldered.
A twilight of smudged sketches
the colors of ochre.
Can I never forgive myself?
This cannot be fixed, made over.
How does one cast off, cut loose, this sea anchor,
this clubbed foot.

As far as choices go, something clearly needs doing.
(Foundering, is that a choice?)

So many dear, dearest ones have, to my surprise,
already had a seat here. Left their essence, and perhaps –
no I'm sure, a message.
It says: *Save nothing – not even yourself.*

Your Voice

It seemed your voice
but I did not seek it
as I have.
Nor move away from it,
as I have.
Was grateful for your presence,
in the emptiness without you.

The Old Man

He's talking about the fire
about ashes being washed away in the rain
carried down rivers to the sea
to the ocean
and to the Milky Way

for Jodo John Candy

The Sweet Spot

Driving to a memorial service for a good friend's younger brother.
We're all getting on now, but he was still the youngest.
Exceedingly smart and quick-witted, he threw himself at his life like
a youngster careening downhill on a ratty bike.
All he knows is faster, all he feels is the wind and the fierce,
sweet activity.
At the very periphery of awareness, too fleeting to give pause, are the
usual cautions, glimmers of apprehension.
The obvious response, we all agreed on that at one time or the other–
faster!
Go faster!
Driving along heading into the tunnel to the city, a flick of movement,
a smudge streaks my windshield.
Once upon an instant ago, an insect was winging its way...
Another service to find room for on the hard Quaker benches.

A Coppery Hue

Ill at ease in the predawn darkness,
looking for ways to improve my lot.
Occasional sounds bounced out of the forest.
Stirrings before the first stirrings,
between the unquiet stillness of night,
and the earliest sounds of transition.

Casting about, penetrating the dark,
it was echoes that were most noticeable.
Echoes all around, miraculously missing solid objects,
never colliding with other sounds.

I slipped inside one, a coppery hue filled it,
and, knee to chin, spun and whirled,
till we disappeared in the coming day.

Easy Love

Holding your hand, how many times have I held it
since mine found yours one afternoon?
You turned away to speak to a friend, and from the
corner of my eye I caught a glimpse, my hand reaching for yours.

At that first touch our fingers found a will of their own,
informing the rest of us, "Look – how easy."
Your head tilted onto my arm as we walked, and you said,
"I love you."
I said, "I love you too."
How easy.

New Music

I almost had it right
an exact combination that worked
now poking along traffic passing
the phrasing evaporated around a curve
and is headed across the wetlands

Farther on she lies no longer expecting anything
still strong healthy except for a couple of things
Death's not even on the parkway yet
we've gone from trying to rearrange the sequence
to simply keeping each other company

Not allowed really
lives played out of sequence
except on these special occasions
I have found egg salad on rye in hospital
cafeterias to be an effective antidote
to the enormity of changing forms
the apparent randomness

Of course
even without a phrase that satisfies
we attend
there is no antidote we have yet to find it
for that snarling thing that works its way up
one's spine
giving a cruel twist at the jaw in passing
then out through chapped lips

And of eyelids caked with Sandman
remember him a little girl's friend
in a kinder darkness
reminding her as she sleeps rolls over
of soft embraces
quilted comforters

GARY GALSWORTH

Sandman – now master of ceremonies in opiate dreams
holding a seat for us in gentle morphine clouds

And so we attend to the children
set aside our squabbles
give over our attention
for what – why bother – for this transformation
so raw
and

And the children have you seen them
I have
ten years hence lined up at Burger King
why bother
it's what we do even as it starts to get the best of us

You'll notice falling behind in traffic
lights flashing past
a loss of conviction in the necessary urgencies
of sequence and consequence

New music enters our range of perception
That's it
now we've got it right

Personally I intend to box all these carefully arranged
dish and train sets for another ten years
at least
now is hardly the time

"Our only recourse may be in keeping better company "
I hope I've got the patience
the guts for it
some do she does
a deft hand
Love's breath mixing with assorted vapors

The gap widens
playing full speed ahead the children
slow down feel a thinning out
they are not alarmed it's just a certain fragility
has cast itself over the world
the taste of brittle morning after a cold night

Empty-handed
a little girl skips past
and through the Sandman's portal

About "New Music"

Yoa Tierney was my daughter's best friend, a sister really. She grew
up to become a truly lovely young woman, a special being. She also
became a doctor and mother of three.
After her third child she caught a breast cancer but did not find out
in time.
In a little over two years, despite the best medicine, she left us
to weep, but also smile and laugh.
This poem is about the last days together.

Quasimodo

Standing with you in the dark
a wordless dark
I feel a heartbeat I'm sure it's yours
I know it's mine
Your warmth drifts over us
and in the darkness
I close my eyes close them tight

An image
pale light appears
relief gratitude wash over me
to find in this lifetime a moment
one moment
this moment

About the Author

Gary Galsworth was born and grew up in the New York City area. After high school, he spent three years in the Marine Corps before attending the Art Institute of Chicago and the University of Chicago, majoring in painting and, later, filmmaking. He made a number of films during the late 60s into the 70s.

A student of Zen and Vipassana Practice going back many years, Gary is also a master plumber (worked with Phillip Glass and other artist/plumbers, way back when).

Poetry began as a quiet aside. One of his oldest poems, "Winter's Passing," is from 1964.

His daughter, Ondine, is a mom, yoga instructor, and writer, living in Hoboken. His son, Danny, is a recent grad. from engineering school near Los Angeles and now works in the Philadelphia area.

Gary lives in Hoboken, New Jersey, spends a good part of his time in an old house in Long Branch on the Jersey Shore, and travels regularly, sometimes to meditation retreats—and often to Providence, Rhode Island to see his significant-other, Carol, a nurse practitioner in a clinic there.

88437076R00102

Made in the USA
Columbia, SC
05 February 2018